AF446776

Monetary Management
for a Free Economy

Monetary Management
for a Free Economy

Alan Jacobs

VANTAGE PRESS
New York

FIRST EDITION

Copyright © 1992 by Alan Jacobs

Published by Vantage Press, Inc.
516 West 34th Street, New York, New York 10001

Manufactured in the United States of America
ISBN: 0-533-10213-8

Library of Congress Catalog Card No.: 92-90679

0 9 8 7 6 5 4 3 2 1

To all whose quality of life is damaged or destroyed by inflation, unemployment, failed business, and other effects of recurring trade cycles—the ultimate horrors of which are civil and international wars.

Contents

Preface

Most people, economists included, accept that the trade cycle of recessions and recoveries, booms and depressions, is inevitable. This is reasonable, given the present state of economic knowledge—and several hundred years of history would seem to say that it is so. Many regard the trade cycle as the penalty for progress that defies all efforts to counteract it.

Certainly, a number of prominent economists have advanced proposals to combat the trade cycle, particularly its most damaging aspects of inflation and unemployment. Time has proven all to fail. But none has attempted the fundamental analysis of successfully understanding the modern use of money in business economies such as ours, economies that basically support the freedoms that we cherish, where individual preferences of consumer demand are allowed to determine what is produced as our economic standards of living.

However, there is nothing inevitable about the trade cycle. Indeed, it is nonsense to suggest that the real exchanges we engage in to improve our quality of life should have any cause for periodic reversals of progress. Every barter exchange, where real value is exchanged for real value without the use of money, is of advantage to both parties. The more exchanges, the greater the advantages; and there are no consequent disadvantages. Using money enables many more real exchanges to be effected than is possible to arrange under barter conditions, but we have not understood the way that we must manage the use of money so that it does not introduce consequent disadvantages—the terrible ravages of the trade cycle.

Economics should not be a complex subject. Only a lack of understanding of the way that our monetary system operates and the way that it must be managed if we are to get its benefits makes it so. This book provides that understanding, so that we may apply this new knowledge to overcome the major problems that currently beset us.

The reason for our poor performance in economics, compared to outstanding successes in the physical sciences, is that we have not done the fundamental analysis. We have not recognised the basically simple patterns of economic behaviour in people that are as constant and unchanging as any natural phenomena upon which the physical sciences base their laws and obtain their solutions. With the right analysis and knowledge, solutions to the management of economic situations become equally possible.

The basic pattern of economics in free societies is that of business activity. Business activity is the total economic activity of using resources to produce our standards of living. Total business employs all of the resources used in economic production, and total business produces all of the goods and services that comprise our economic standards of living. Business economies react to circumstances in exactly the same way that individual businesses do, because economy reactions are nothing more or less than the sum of all individual business reactions.

The concept of total business and the impetus that causes total business to operate at certain levels are of absolute importance in economics. They are the key to the way that we must manage our monetary system; it is only the lack of proper monetary understanding and management in business economies that gives rise to trade cycles.

Money incomes paid by individual businesses for supply can be spent as demand over the production of all businesses, so total supply and total demand can only be properly related through managing money flows at the level of total business.

The way that money is currently used in economic activity completely separates demand from supply. It causes new supply to match current demand—however deficient or excessive that demand may be, even for current supply. Money demand must be managed through our monetary system so that its total is always just sufficient to promote or maintain total supply at the level of full employment. Only by recognising the behaviour patterns that achieve this can economic standards of living be maximised for all.

Total business is simply the sum of all individual business activity. It functions just like any business because it is the sum of all business transactions and decisions. It expands and contracts in response to the same criteria that cause any business to expand or contract in trying to maximise its return on the equity funds invested, i.e., its rate of profit relative to alternative rewards that may be available. Only a satisfactory relative rate of profit for total business will see the level of business activity achieve and maintain full employment.

The completely different functions of funds, first as a means of facilitating business activity and second as a medium of exchange, have not been properly analysed and understood. Nor is it understood—because funds are facilitating, nonproductive resources—that interest, profits, and taxes are transfers of income, not additions to total income.

This work can only be assessed from fundamentals, not from current economic knowledge, which has many faults in logic. If you believe that people try to make exchanges and investments to their best advantage and would like to have the social and economic environment in which to maximise their quality of life, you will not be able to fault this analysis or solution. You will see how wrong current economic teaching is. It will be shown how damaging it is to attempt to fight inflation with artificially high rates of interest. And how economically futile it is to expect to combat inflation when wage rates are increased because of price rises that have been caused by previously increased wage rates!

These measures only aggravate inflation, unemployment, and the other evils of existing trade-cycle conditions.

Monetary Management
for a Free Economy

Chapter 1
Introduction

What Economics Is

Economics is the study of the exchanges made between people for the purpose of providing themselves with better economic standards of living. The aim of studying economics is to establish the conditions under which people can manage their exchanges in the way that allows them to maximise their individual economic standards of living in any given circumstances.

The study involves analysing what economic standards of living consist of, what economic activity is, what given circumstances have to be considered, what facilities may be used to assist, and what rules need to be made to manage those facilities, so that efforts are best rewarded.

What Economics Is Not

Economics is not the study of self-sufficiency, of growing tomatoes for home use, of self-building the family home, or of the pleasure gained from playing the piano, no matter how much these contribute to the quality of life. Only transactions that involve exchanges with other people are studied; these may include buying tomato seedlings, purchasing bricks for the home, and paying for lessons on the piano. If we were all totally self-sufficient without exchanges, there would be no economics to study.

Economics is not the study of wealth, of who owns how much of whatever exists at any time. This is taken in economics as one of the given circumstances. If, for any reason, it is thought that there should be a change in the ownership or distribution of wealth, this is a matter for social consideration, not economic.

Economics is not about scarcity, except to divide the world into nature and everything else—with nature being freely available to everybody and everything else being scarce. Economics is concerned only with everything else; at every stage, nature and its effects are accepted as given. Initially, nature included everything except people. As soon as people claimed ownership of, or applied their labour to, nature, the product ceased to be freely available to everybody and is no longer classed as nature. It has an exchangeable value; nature does not.

Economics is not the study of laws and taxes, which must also be taken as given. These are imposed upon communities by their governments, hopefully elected to look after the social interests of people. Exchanges must operate within, and make the best of, any framework of laws and taxes that exists. The government budget of tax revenue and spending on administration and welfare is a social reckoning, not a mechanism for economic management.

Nor is economics concerned whether behaviour is considered to be ethical or not. Economics must study what exists. For example, price control may exist through laws that are passed. It may or may not be considered ethical to observe those laws, depending on one's involvement. Where price control applies, a person having to sell for less is likely to have a different attitude from a person who can buy for less, and perhaps from a person who would like to pay more if only he could get supply. Also, products that by law are declared ethically undesirable may still be produced and sold; economics must recognise this activity.

Economic Standards of Living

Improved economic standards of living relate to each person involved in making exchanges. These exchanges are mostly made on behalf of families—father, mother, children—sometimes others, sometimes just the one person. However, future reference will be made only to the principals making the exchanges, even though others may have contributed to the decisions. Sometimes Dad earns the income and Mum does the spending—each is a principal.

The economic standard of living for each person is the net result of satisfactions from the goods and services received in exchange for the willing sacrifices made to obtain them. The goods and services include food, clothing, shelter, health services, education, transport, entertainment, etc.—everything that may now be purchased with money. Sacrifices are now virtually limited to the supply of owned resources that can be sold for money.

Economic standard of living must not be confused with total standard of living, or quality of life. The latter includes, in addition to economic standard of living, all leisure-time activities, such as family life, sports, games, recreations, religious observances, social and charitable activities, etc. It also includes the idle time of unemployment and any activity that may arise as a consequence of enforced idleness. For the purposes of study, all noneconomic standard of living activity in the quality of life is classed as social standard of living.

A quality of life may have widely differing requirements for economic content, depending upon each person's preferences. The study of economics must accept these as given. However, unless persons have at least minimum economic standards of living, it is unlikely that they will enjoy good quality of life. This may lead to antisocial behaviour that impacts on the quality of other lives.

A higher economic standard of living, for no change in the

sacrifices needed to obtain it, will result in a higher quality of life for that person. This is not true beyond the point where more leisure is preferred to more time spent in earning income. Nor is the quality of life higher when some leisure time would prefer to be sacrificed for employment and income.

Economic standards of living are not described in terms of wealth of assets or funds, though there is usually a correlation between wealth and living standards. A person owning many assets, or even in receipt of a good money income, could have a relatively poor economic standard of living if very little were spent on new goods and services. It is not a function of economics to change the distribution of wealth in a community, no matter how desirable this may seem to be. If changes are desired, this is a social matter for government legislation, and, presumably, taxes on wealth for the benefit of those who are poor.

Economic Activity

Economic activity today is the sacrifice of resources used in production, exchanged for the satisfaction of the goods and services produced. All standard-of-living sacrifices are made for money incomes, and all satisfactions are purchased for money prices. This activity is conducted as business, whereby money incomes are paid for resources used, and money prices are received for resultant production.

This was not always the case. Until the Industrial Revolution introduced large-scale employment and production, much of economic activity was the exchange of commodities for commodities. Individual or small groups of farmers, tradesmen, and others produced their own specialty goods and services, and exchanged them between themselves, or for other commodities like sheep, wheat, or gold, to the advantage of each. Even the larger scale operations of landlords were on the basis of farmer tenants providing goods and services in exchange for the right to obtain a living from the rented land. Of course, there was some direct employment of labour to produce goods and services, but usually for consumption by the employer rather than for exchange.

Economics today must, therefore, study what resources people sacrifice to production and exchange, and how that production and exchange is effected, so that each person's preferences for an economic standard of living can be best met. This must allow for the opportunity to maximise the quality of life, by allowing for leisure time at the stage where more goods and services are not the preferred choice.

The Economic Environment

Economics is concerned with making the best of exchange activity for each and every person; this means that the environment in which exchanges take place is everything else but individual people. Environment includes all of nature, the population of people, real capital, the system and facilities used for production and exchanges, international trade and finance, and the social system of laws, government administration, and taxes. Most of this environment may be taken as given—at least in the short term, because it rarely changes significantly in that time.

Nature is everything that is not owned, directly or indirectly, through businesses or government, by people. It is, therefore, available free of any people sacrifice or charge to the production and exchange process. However, the use of nature in production in a way that is not renewable, either by nature or by production, may well represent a loss to the quality of many lives in this or future generations, and may need social laws for its protection. Nature includes the weather of good seasons and bad, storms, floods, earthquakes, fires, pestilence, and not-owned land, sea, air, minerals, oil, forests, fishes, etc. When a natural resource becomes owned by people, and therefore subject to sacrifice if used, it is no longer classed as nature.

The bountifulness of nature, or the lack of it, is extremely important in the production process, and largely determines whether a region becomes economically rich or poor. Desirable things that can be owned, like minerals, oil, and forests, often pass out of being nature through ownership, but seasons and natural disasters are still well beyond people control. What is still nature, and not protected by laws, must be disregarded as a sacrifice or cost to the production process, despite its profound influence on output. Nature originally provides all of the materials and much of the services, in production output.

People themselves change very little in the short term, although in the longer term, education, new knowledge, improved foods, and nutrition have their effects on each person's skill and ability. On the other hand, population preferences sometimes change very rapidly when new products become available at prices that many would like to pay—railway transport, motor cars, telephones, and television sets are a few instances through time. The demand for such additional goods and services may mean that many people would prefer to sacrifice some of their accustomed leisure, i.e., they would now prefer to work longer hours for more income to purchase more goods and services. Economic knowledge must be able to let business practice adjust to such changed circumstances.

Real capital is everything used in production that exists at the start of a period and is owned by people. Natural resources owned by people are real capital. Every produced thing that exists at the start of a period must have originally come from nature in earlier production periods. Real capital includes land, buildings, plant, equipment, tools, etc. It will be discussed in more detail later.

The system used for production and exchanges in a free economy is called business. Business activity is central to economic study. Business purchases the use of nonequity resources from people for money incomes, combines productive resources into goods and services, and sells resultant output to people for prices. Any excess of prices over nonequity incomes and taxes paid accrues to suppliers of equity resources as profit incomes.

As explained earlier this system did not always exist, but is a consequence of the Industrial Revolution and the use of facilities to manage production and exchanges to better advantage. Unfortunately, the system has always had a lack of understanding of the use of money in business activity, which has persisted to this day. This causes business, or trade, cycle conditions of recessions and recoveries. These cause untold misery through unemployment, loss of production, lowered economic standards of living, and to many the destruction of the quality of life itself. A main aim of present economics must be to remove the cause of business cycles. There is no logical reason why they should exist in the production and exchange process.

International trade and finance is a significant part of the economic environment. It is the means whereby people in countries of differing natural and people environments can each improve their lots through trade. Unfortunately again, a loss of sight of this basic purpose has seen international trade and finance become the tail that wags the dog in efforts to overcome the lack of knowledge of the business cycle. This subject will be left until knowledge of how to obviate business cycles is available to domestic economies.

All economic activity operates in an overriding environment of social laws, administered by government enforcement and financial budgets. The latter collect taxes and borrow money for redistribution as welfare and for expenditure to operate their instrumentalities. Economics must try to make the most of our standards of living in any social environment. Taxation requirements will, of course, be less when fewer people need social welfare because unemployment is lower. Unemployment is obviously a waste of productive potential, as well as being shattering to the quality of many lives.

Chapter 2
Economic Resources

Labour

Suppose you found yourself on an uninhabited island or in Stone Age conditions with no possessions and no contact with the outside world. How would you survive, i.e., how would you get a standard of living? Only by applying the use of your labour to whatever nature had to offer. You may be able to pick fruit, carry water, build a shelter, make a spear to hunt and fish, etc. There is no productive resource that you could apply to nature other than labour. Whilst results would depend significantly on what nature had to offer, there is nothing that you could obtain other than through the use of labour.

Nothing has changed, nor can it ever change. The only way that people today can produce standards of living is by applying their labour to freely available nature, whether they live in primitive or developed communities. Labour is the only basic factor of production that people can supply; freely available nature provides everything else. Labour, is therefore, the only basic income and cost of production. All other incomes and costs must ultimately be transfers out of labour's contribution to production.

Real Capital

In making a spear, labour is applied to nature, not for immediate use, but to enable labour to perform better when used in conjunction with the spear later on. The spear, and even surplus food from yesterday saved until today, are real capital. Only things subsequently consumed, used in production or whose services provide or assist in production, qualify as real capital; other things are of no economic use or value. Of course, something that is only looked at to provide consumer satisfaction still qualifies.

Although the sacrifices to produce real capital are made before its use, the cost of real capital for reckoning purposes may be held over (capitalised) in the periods of its production and applied (depreciated) in the periods of its use or consumption. This transfer of costs is generally acceptable, because the benefits to new production come in the periods of the use of real capital, rather than in the periods of its production. No new production now takes place without the use of labour that is improved by at least some real capital.

Real capital is not an independent factor of production. Its existence arose originally from the use of labour applied to nature, and it is now only productive when used in combination with labour. Real capital without labour cannot, and will never, produce anything—no matter how automated some factories get. It simply allows labour to perform better—in fact, very much better.

Real capital has developed through the ages, rapidly increasing the productivity of labour with its use. Its contribution through time is so great that its cost cannot be referenced all the way back to the original labour costs. We account in periods of time, not in time to date, so real capital, through depreciation, is a period cost of production. It is a transfer of costs from the periods of its production to the periods of its use. Real capital-improved labour is the only period productive resource.

Because improved labour is the only basic productive resource and cost, and depreciation of real capital is predetermined, wages relative to business productivity establish the real value of money for a period. Current wage rates determine whether that real value is different from the previous period. If it is different, changing the real value of money breaks the relationship that depreciation is meant to provide for the recovery of money previously spent on real capital. Business then has to provide for the changed replacement cost of real capital, not its past or actual cost. This may not be recognised by, for example, taxing authorities, which may allow only historical costs for the calculation of taxable profits. It also causes problems of accounting, because businesses account in money, not real terms.

The suppliers of labour and real capital could lay claim to the only real incomes in a period. However, we shall see that there are other transfers of income. These are for the use of two facilitating resources: funds and the social environment. Wages, depreciation, the costs of using funds and money, and the tax costs comprise total costs of production. In a business economy, they also represent total prices and total incomes. There are no costs of production for total business that cannot be allocated to one of these headings.

Funds and Money

Whilst real capital has provided the means for increasing the productivity of labour, funds have provided the facility for using potential productivity, and for making potential exchanges, to allow that level of increase in our standards of living. Funds are not a period productive resource like labour and real capital, because they do not of themselves, or in combination, produce anything. But funds are used to facilitate both the bringing together of labour and real capital in production and, as money, in the making of exchanges. These separate functions need to be clearly identified to understand how the use of funds as money must be managed, so that we may get the advantages, without the disadvantages that come from misuse.

In a modern economy, funds are used as money to purchase all resources used in production. Funds come from the banking system. They are debts in money terms, and of course every debt (amount owed by) has an equal credit (amount owed to), which makes their overall total absolutely zero. For example, every bank deposit is a debt owed by a bank to a depositor. With a total of zero, it is not hard to understand that funds do not contribute to production and that associated incomes are transfers from productive incomes.

Banks operate on the principle that they may lend amounts to others, who effect that borrowing by drawing cheques, e.g., to purchase resources to be used in production, or for numerous other reasons. Drawn cheques, when presented at the bank, give rise to both a debit (to the drawer) and a credit (to the depositor). It is quite coincidental whether the presenting of a cheque increases the amount of a bank's deposits (debts to others) or decreases the amount of its loans (debts by others). Nor does it matter; the absolute level of the debt side of funds, mostly bank deposits, is of no economic significance (despite the claims of monetarist economists).

Whether funds exist at banks, or are created by them, all that matters is the amount of funds that is actually spent on incomes by purchasing the use of resources, and the amount that is spent on prices by purchasing the resultant production of goods and services. Only these amounts of funds become, for the time being, medium-of-exchange money.

Money today is nominally used as a medium in the exchange of resources used for resultant production. Because any money paid as incomes for resources used may be applied to the purchase of any resultant production, the real economic exchange in a period must be regarded for monetary management purposes as one big exchange—total resources used for total resultant production. The money exchange is total incomes for total prices, complicated by two facts: presale incomes influence prices, and prices determine remainder incomes.

The failure to recognise the totality of the real exchange that the use of money introduces, and the need to measure and control the total use of money as a medium of exchange in each productive period so that a constant real value obtains, is the major cause of economic problems.

As with any medium, money has no quantity. Money is created when funds are spent on incomes and absorbed back into funds when spent on goods and services. Speech as a medium of communication is created when words are spoken and absorbed when words are heard. Words spoken but not heard do not act as a medium of communication, any more than money paid as income but not spent as prices acts as a medium of exchange.

When part of income is saved and banked, the bank has a right and an obligation to ensure that that money is spent on goods and services. If this does not happen, money is not functioning as a medium of exchange. Banks, however, do not always know what amounts lent will be spent on. Funds may be used to purchase production, to pay incomes, to repay other debt, or to purchase securities.

Banks receive funds when businesses sell production. They also make funds available (within certain limits) on the security of real capital, or purely out of credit creation—and again those funds may be spent in any way. They may receive foreign funds from overseas or be required to send funds abroad. There is no effort made to identify savings out of incomes and to ensure that money savings are spent on goods and services. To a bank, it is of little or no consequence in economic terms, what funds are spent on.

Funds are needed to pay money incomes, because businesses

using resources do not raise IOUs against their expected production. Spending of money as prices on resultant production comes from money incomes and funds, not from specific IOUs that were raised, and need to be redeemed, against production. Sales revenue goes into the pool of funds available for future use. As a result the use of funds as money must be measured and controlled for both incomes and prices, if money is to maintain a constant real value through time.

An alternative approach to the use of common money could see each business issue its own IOUs as incomes and accept only its own IOUs as prices. This would have an enormous problem of standardisation of real value across all businesses—or of needing rates of exchange between the money units of IOUs issued by different businesses. The method existed in part for a while in some places.

The use of funds adds nothing to production from the use of any given labour and real capital; it just allows more labour and real capital to be joined in production than would otherwise be the case. The cost of funds used is, in effect, a transfer from the earning capacity of improved labour to the suppliers of funds for the facility of being able to arrange more production.

Of course, because the use of funds greatly facilitates production and exchanges, the real return to labour, with depreciation already predetermined, is far better than if funds were not used. Nevertheless, it must be recognised that the cost of using funds is a part of prices and therefore a sharing of the real income that improved labour generates. Using funds is a transfer of income; it is not additional income or an additional real cost. Because using funds facilitates greater total production, the cost is not a net loss to wages. But the amount paid for the cost of funds does directly affect the immediate real return to wages.

The quantity of funds at any one time is better calculated by knowing the totals of borrowed and equity funds used by business, rather than by totalling its opposite side of bank deposits, etc., which may include amounts that are not used by business. Funds borrowed by governments also earn income, but this income is paid out of taxation, not directly out of prices.

The history of money is interesting but not very enlightening with respect to the current situation, although our sins of omission probably arise from not updating our thinking to modern times. The first monies were commodities that were commonly acceptable as means of dual exchanges. Wheat, cattle, gold, silver, etc., were often intermediate trades between the resources or commodities that were the final objects of the exchanges. As such, commodity monies were usually referred to as mediums of exchange. This was a wrong use of the term and a misconception of commodity money.

All of those intermediate trades were complete real exchanges—virtually barter in that they gave real value for real value—even when gold and silver took the form of coins. It did not matter that the second part of an intended dual exchange was not completed, because each party held real value from the first exchange, whether in commodities or commodity money. Commodity money was also described as a store of value, which it was, because it could be used for later exchanges of commodity money for commodities at the same real value.

After the Industrial Revolution, and particularly after abandoning the gold standard, the making of exchanges and the use of money took different forms. Modern societies have now completely abandoned any trading of commodities for commodities, and there are no exchanges of commodities for commodity money or vice versa. They now trade only resources used for commodities, using funds for money in what we call business activity.

Social Environment

Having a social environment of government is a democratic

right enjoyed by people in free economies. The costs of government administration in providing and upholding a constitution, associated laws, public works, roads, and common services like defence and law enforcement, include use of the same resource types as for the business activity of producing and exchanging our economic standards of living. However, because the output of this social production is not sold and does not add to our economic standards of living, the suppliers of social-use resources would seem to be without claim to incomes to provide them with their living standards. This is remedied by the government levying taxes on the business use of resources and sales, and paying equivalent incomes out of taxes to suppliers.

The government budget of taxation and expenditure on administration goes further. It collects more taxes to provide incomes or income supplements on a welfare basis for various reasons—disabilities, unemployment, child endowment, health and hospital subsidisation, etc.

Where government expenditure is budgeted to exceed tax revenue, usually for expenditure of a capital nature, funds are borrowed, and the cost of funds amortised over the life of the national asset. The sinking-fund payment is charged to the revenue budget in much the same way as depreciation and interest on funds are charged as costs against business production.

Not all taxes that the law imposes are levied by governments. For example, copyrights, patents, and royalties are simply legal rights to levy private taxes.

Chapter 3
Economic Activity

Business Production and Sales

Business buys things, adds value, and sells things. The things that business buys are resources, the value it adds is by combining those resources with nature, and the things that it sells are the goods and services of resultant production.

By defining business as the use of resources and sale of resultant production, it follows that all economic activity is business activity. And because we recognise economic activity as business activity, we can now find the cause of, and the cure for, the economic problems that arise out of the lack of monetary understanding and management.

Business activity is operated by people as individuals or in groups as partners, corporations, and public bodies. Businesses use funds to buy intermediate goods and services from other businesses (purchases) and to buy or obtain labour and real capital resources provided by people to combine into productivity and achieve production. Then they sell the produced goods and services to other businesses (intermediate sales) or to people (final sales).

Businesses are the only employers of resources used in economic production, and the only producers and sellers of economic production. Productive resources employed comprise the use of labour, the use of real capital, and nature. Real capital includes every existing thing used in production that is owned by people (directly or through businesses), whether natural (land), produced and not consumed (stock), or produced and not used up (plant). The new goods and services of business production constitute our entire economic standards of living.

Purchases and sales of things existing at the start of a period, e.g., real capital and documents, such as shares, debentures, bank deposits, etc., whether those things are used in business or not, are simply legal transfers of ownership. The things exchanged have no effect upon the employment of resources or upon new production. Of course, if resources are used in effecting a transaction, those resources (e.g., agents' selling) are new production.

Business activity is total economic activity. The level of the economic employment of resources, and the level of our economic standards of living, depend entirely upon the amount and continuation of business activity.

Social Production and Distribution

Social activity also buys things and adds value, but does not sell resultant production. Instead it distributes production on social or political bases. Production is, mainly, of services, e.g., government administration, defence, law enforcement, etc. This secondary purchase of resources is paid for out of taxes on business activity, and the transfers of purchasing power enable the resource providers to share in purchases of business production for their standards of living. Production not for sale adds to our social, not to our economic, standards of living.

Taxes are also used to provide purchasing power to recipients of social welfare on the basis of needs. No production is involved (administration is included in the previous paragraph).

Resources Used in Business Activity

The only period productive resources employed for reward by business in a period are those provided by people—use of labour and use of real capital. All original materials and some nonpeople services and events are provided free of charge by nature. Funds used to facilitate production and exchange are also provided by people, such as bank depositors and shareholders. Use of labour, real capital, funds, and social environment are the total resources used in, and the total costs of, business production.

Productivity

Labour and real capital have been identified as the only period productive resources outside of freely available nature. Productivity within an economic environment depends, therefore, entirely upon the use of these two resources; the effects of nature on productivity in determining resultant production just have to be accepted as inevitable. The activity of total business consists of applying productivity to nature. In the case of individual businesses, or periods of time, productivity is applied also to intermediate products, the stocks of which count as real capital.

Despite the fact that labour is the only basic productive resource, labour today has no significant productivity of its own. Real capital has none at all. The combined productivity of labour and real capital, as improved labour, is a vital concept in the understanding and management of a business economy. Productivity must be defined in such a way that it can be measured and related to money flows for incomes and prices. Otherwise, for monetary management purposes, we cannot know how much money demand must be for it to be related to productivity.

Productivity cannot be related to output of resultant production, because this is dependent upon nature and results are unknown. In any case, the diversity of goods and services produced is so wide and changeable that no means for real measuring is possible. By relating productivity to its component resources of labour and real capital, however, measurement becomes relatively easy.

For any given total quantity of labour and real capital used, output depends, at least in the short to medium term, upon the number of hours that are worked. If businesses average 40 hours work a week and 40 million units of output are produced, then working 38 or 42 hours would produce 38 or 42 million units respectively. In any business, if 0 hours are worked, or even if 0 labour or 0 real capital were used with any quantity of the other, output would be 0. Of course, results for any one business may not be exactly on average for total business. Also, for any one person or production team, there are limits to the hours per week that can be worked effectively. The environment of industrial law generally precludes such situations, and wide-of-the-mark exceptions are not a consideration here.

When the potential output of real capital per hour worked is increased relative to its labour requirement, productivity rises proportionately for each hour worked. This has been the basis for increasing standards of living ever since the Industrial Revolution, both by increasing the production of goods and services and by reducing the number of hours worked to obtain them. Whilst the money cost of the potential of real capital is not necessarily proportional to that potential in any one instance, overall this is likely to be true, at least in the short term. Longer term, new techniques tend towards reduced money costs per unit of potential.

It is proposed that, in the short term, productivity can best be measured as the product or multiplication of the quantity of labour hours worked times the amount of real capital cost. In the longer term, this can be adjusted by factors for the quality of labour and the quality of real capital, each expressed as a percentage of a base year. It is not suggested that this will necessarily give good figures for any one business, but that over all businesses it will be very reliable—and the best that is available. After all, productivity per employee increases by an average of about 2 percent per annum in developed countries. Even using this index times the total number in full-time employment would give a reasonable approximation of productivity. There is no basis for saying that productivity cannot be adequately measured. Of course, nature must be excluded from the calculation of productivity or the measure serves no purpose.

It must be borne in mind that productivity is related to input and costs, and not to the market values and profits of individual businesses. It is only when total business is being considered, when total costs and total final sales become identical, that the relationship between productivity and demand is important.

The Use of Money in Business

The cost of labour is called wages. All references to wages include all payments to people for the use of labour such as salaries, holiday pay, sick leave, annual leave, long service leave, superannuation, workers compensation, termination pay, etc. Wage rates are wages divided by hours worked. The cost of nonequity funds is called interest. The cost of equity funds is called profit. Taxes are amounts levied as the result of any private or government legal rights.

The way that business activity operates is that businesses finance the payment of wages, interest, taxes, and purchases from other businesses in advance of sales revenue by obtaining equity and nonequity funds. In primary industries, the combined efforts of labour and real capital (which combination is called productivity) are applied to nature. In secondary industries, productivity is applied mainly to intermediate goods that have been purchased from other businesses. In tertiary industries, productivity is mainly in the form of services for people. Resultant production is sold.

For an individual business, the excess of intermediate and final sale amounts over purchases, wages, depreciation, interest, and taxes accrues as profit to equity capital. For total business, where purchases and sales between businesses cancel out exactly, the excess of final sales value over wages, depreciation, interest, and taxes accrues as profit to total equity capital. There are no items of business expenditure that do not fall into one of these categories.

Of course the basic exchange process means that suppliers of resources and rights to business are the only ones entitled to share the resultant production of business. Our society already recognises this by the fact that all of sales revenue accrues as income—wages to labour, interest to nonequity funds, depreciation to real capital, taxes to governments and other holders of rights, and the remainder of prices as profit to equity funds. Incomes nominally can purchase all of resultant production.

But this does not take into account the effects of the time lag between the business purchases and the sales of production. This may be anything from minutes to, more often, weeks, months and years. Consider the time it takes for mined iron ore and coal to become motor cars, whose steel probably includes the bodies of other cars scrapped after years of use.

Because incomes may be spent on any production of any business in any time period, one effect of this time lag is that there may be no relationship between the real value of money for incomes and the real value of money for prices in their different time periods. Another effect is that we allow more or less funds than were paid or expected to be paid as incomes to be spent on production, thereby changing prices and profits. As a result, prices and profits when received are distorted relative to the prepaid incomes of wages and interest earned in that production. These had been paid for at rates that were expected to retain their real values.

Our use of money provides no measurement of what is paid for labour and nonequity funds through time, no control of payments relative to the quantities of those resources used, no measurement or control of final sales amounts, and therefore no measurement or control over the return to equity capital for the quantity used. Although we pay lip-service to total incomes being equal to total prices, we do not ensure that those who earn either prepaid or postpaid incomes receive real value for their money, i.e., that their money can buy what they expected to be able to buy when it was earned.

Because there is no measurement or control, it is not possible for unmanaged total payments for prepaid resources to maintain a constant relationship to the productivity of those resources, so there must always be COST inflation or deflation of money incomes for wages, depreciation, and interest. Nor is it possible for unmanaged total final spending to maintain a constant relationship to productivity, so there must always be DEMAND inflation or deflation of the prices of the goods and services that comprise our economic standards of living. And, most importantly, there must always be an exaggerated effect on profits relative to equity capital used, because any difference in final sales value gives that same absolute difference to profits, which are, of course, much smaller in size than sales.

For example, if profits are 5 percent of sales, a 1 percent change in sales value gives a 20 percent change in profits for no change in equity capital—should sales decrease from $100 to $99, profits decrease from $5 to $4. When sales decrease from $100 to $95, profits vanish altogether.

The Level of Business Activity

The factor that determines whether a business, and therefore in total all business, expands or contracts its level of employment in productive activity is the rate of profit achieved on equity funds relative to any alternate use of those funds. The only alternatives are the business or government use of funds, both at the rate of interest, so the critical factor is average rate of business profit relative to the rate of interest.

Not all of equity funds are available for alternate use, even though some rates of profit are unfavourable. Most equity funds are tied up in business, having been used to purchase real capital assets or used as working capital. Rarely is it possible to sell installed production equipment at anything like its original cost. Generally the only funds that become available for alternate use are period depreciation recoveries, when decisions have to be made whether or not to reinvest these in replacement real capital. With depreciation recoveries mostly running at rates of 5 to 15 percent per annum of asset values, the number of businesses deciding not to reinvest all of these funds in real capital becomes very significant so far as the future level of business activity is concerned. For every 1 percent reduction in the level of reinvestment in business activity, employment, production, and living standards will decline by 1 percent.

Although it is the relative profitability of equity capital that is critical for the future level of business activity, it does not much matter whether business uses equity or nonequity funds—so long as the total in use remains the same. The transfer from equity funds to nonequity funds in business, because business rates of interest are more attractive than rates of profit, may mean shifts in production from some businesses to others, but it will not mean reduced production. It is when funds transfer to nonbusiness (social) use, or are absorbed in debt reduction, that reduced business activity occurs.

Shifts of funds from business to nonbusiness use occur when government rates of interest become more attractive than rates of profit or business rates of interest. The rates that government is prepared to pay are entirely in the hands of government treasuries or their banking agents. They can offer rates of interest slightly less favourable or slightly more favourable than business rates as a matter of monetary policy to control the level of business employment.

If there is unemployment in the economy, they should offer "low" rates of interest on government loans to steer available funds back into business production. If there is a tendency to overemployment (which has not been evident for many years), they should offer "high" rates of interest on government loans to take some pressure off the business use of funds.

The question then arises as to whether using the rate of interest on government loans to control the level of employment will upset the government's capital works program by providing too few or too many funds. This will not happen, for two reasons. First, the government's other source of funds, taxation, can be used if necessary to offset any shortfall of borrowed funds. Second, there is such a pool of national debt existent that any surplus funds can easily be used to repay old debt. It is just a matter of balancing revenues between current (taxation) and capital (loan) sources, depending on total needs. Lower rates of interest (and higher taxes) should come at times when unemployment is tending to rise.

Chapter 4
Inflation

Types

In a business economy, where resources are exchanged for production through the medium of money, there are two places where inflation or deflation may occur. One is in the exchange of resources for incomes where cost inflation or deflation may occur, and the other is in the exchange of prices for production where demand inflation or deflation may occur.

Of the resources that are exchanged for incomes, real capital has already been paid for. The recovery this period of depreciation is based on past costs, so depreciation income provides no avenue for cost inflation this period. Interest, profit, and tax incomes are transfer incomes and costs only, so that leaves wages as the only source of cost inflation—which it is. Increases in wage rates, i.e., increases in the total costs of labour relative to productivity, are the sole source of cost inflation.

Prices paid for production will cause demand inflation or deflation, provided there is no cost inflation or deflation, when total prices are not a constant multiple of productivity. When there is cost inflation, the multiple must be increased by that margin to determe whether it is demand inflation or deflation that exists.

Although there is much talk about inflation as such, the term has little or no meaning unless preceded by its type of cost or demand. It is not sensible to combine the two and come up with a concept of net inflation, even though this is mostly what is done. Cost inflation causes prices to rise by the increase in wage rates, discounted for increases in productivity. Demand deflation—and it is demand deflation that exists, not demand inflation, whenever there is increasing unemployment—does not cause prices to fall. What happens is that cost inflation causes rates of interest to rise by about that margin, and sales revenues, even at cost inflation prices, leave average rates of profit below real rates of interest. Future use of resources and production is reduced, but prices remain, as they must to try to restore profitability, at cost inflation levels.

The Consumer Price Index

A Consumer Price Index can never be a satisfactory measure of "net" inflation, not only because such a concept is worthless, but also because it contains elements that are totally beyond control. One can never tell from a CPI whether cost or demand inflation has occurred or not, making it virtually useless as an indicator to reflect control action.

There are three reasons for this. First, all prices are subject to the effects of nature on productivity, and nature is totally beyond human control. Nature can and does cause resultant production to be considerably greater or smaller than average expectations. Good seasons and bad have these effects. Very good seasons, droughts, floods, pestilence, and other natural disasters exaggerate them. Better than average production causes prices and a CPI to fall; worse than average production causes prices and a CPI to rise—regardless of any cost or demand inflation or any control action.

Second, all prices are subject to the influences of overseas prices on things that are exported or imported, and overseas prices are completely beyond local control. When significant imported or exported items, like oil, are included in a CPI, again changes have an exaggerated effect on the CPI regardless of any cost or demand inflation or any control action.

The third reason for a CPI not to be able to satisfactorily indicate whether cost or demand inflation exists is that it contains only a weighted selection of prices and does not necessarily reflect the general level of prices. The product and weighting content of each CPI is frequently changed in recognition of this. Every such change breaks the continuity of the measure and is another reason why comparisons with other periods are rarely worthwhile.

Problems

Some of the conditions that falls in the real value of money bring with it are:

(a) people who lend funds are unfairly disadvantaged when repayment is made in funds of lower purchasing power. For example, amounts equal to a weekly living wage invested in an insurance policy or superannuation scheme fifty years ago will now barely buy a retiree a cup of coffee.
(b) people who borrow are unfairly advantaged when repayment is made in funds of lower purchasing power.
(c) current lenders during times of cost inflation require higher rates of interest as some compensation for the loss of value of their funds. Higher rates of interest then become a problem to borrowers for home ownership and business, leading to business failures, repossessions, and unemployment.

(d) cost inflation involves changes in wage and interest rates and in the prices of all goods and services; the frequent changes in rates and prices make for great inefficiency, wasting resources and creating much ill will to lower people's qualities of life. Also, governments take advantage of inflation through progressive rates to increase taxes as a proportion of incomes.

(e) meaningful accounting or statistical analyses in times of changes in the real value of money are almost impossible. The potential of techniques to improve the understanding of market conditions, and so direct resources to best advantage, is largely lost.

Definition

The real value for money is best defined in terms of total spending (which of course equals total incomes) relative to the total productivity of labour and real capital. A constant real value for money (no cost or demand inflation or deflation) exists when total prices and incomes are a constant multiple of total productivity.

The effects of nature on production are thus excluded. The effects of international trade are excluded when there is no change to total productivity because the real value of imports on current account is the same as exports, and there is no change to money flows because of a balance of payments on current account. Measurement and control of rates of exchange for current-account balancing is recommended as a necessary part of monetary management in later chapters.

This definition says that there is no cost or demand inflation when the general level of prices remains unchanged with average conditions of nature and no change in the terms of trade. Incomes for any individual resource and prices for any individual product may change, but there is no change in the real value of money when the general level of prices remains unchanged under these circumstances. Worse than average conditions of nature, or unfavourable movement in the terms of trade, will cause the price level to rise without causing change in the real value of money.

Price rises and falls that are due to nature or overseas conditions are said not to lower or raise the real value of money. The real value of money is established when total incomes are committed relative to the total productivity used by business. The real value of total productivity must be translated to the real value of total production, regardless of whether total production is more or less than the expectation of productivity. Total productivity is expected total real value; total production is actual total real value. The latter in real terms must be the same as the former, because the sacrifice of resources must equal the satisfaction of the production for the exchanges to take place.

A loan of funds equalling forty hours of labour (using certain real capital equipment) in an average season may represent power to purchase 100 units of goods and services. If that loan is repaid in a bad season, and there is no inflation, the funds may be able to purchase only 95 units of goods and services, but this would still represent the purchasing power of the same forty hours of labour. On the other hand, if repaid in a good season, the funds, and forty hours of labour, may be able to purchase 105 units of goods and services. If repaid in another average season, the funds would be able to purchase 100 units of goods and services. In each case the funds could purchase forty hours of improved labour, which is a measurable quantity of real value for monetary management purposes, whereas units of goods and services that differ in product and preference day by day is not a measurable quantity unless a constant real value for money already applies.

A constant real value of money for all incomes must represent a constant real value of money for all prices. Total money spent is the same, and each is total and equal real value when the exchanges are negotiated. Only uncontrollable nature and terms of trade can change the general level of prices when a constant real value for money exists.

Chapter 5
The Rate of Interest

The Rate of Interest and Inflation

Use of the rate of interest as a tool to control the level of employment in business economies is known to be basically correct, even by those who do not fully understand and, consequently, misuse it. Its misuse results from two popular misconceptions amongst economists. One is that higher rates of interest control inflation. The other is that higher rates must be used to attract overseas funds to bridge the gap left by an excess of imports on current account. Each of these fallacies will be dealt with in turn.

The misconception about inflation comes from the beliefs that higher rates of interest reduce money demand, and that the cost inflation of higher wages will be offset by the reduced demand. Higher rates will, of course, lower profits and cause unemployment—for which economists are very sorry, but, they say, these are the recessions we must have!

It is known that total prices give rise to equal total incomes, because profits are the remainder of prices after wages, depreciation, taxes, and interest. In this exchange, wages establish the real value of money, and demand determines whether that real value is maintained for prices, taxes, depreciation, interest, and profits. What is not recognised is that interest and profits, which together are the cost of funds, are complementary incomes. Raise one and the other is lowered. Raising interest charges to business lowers profits, leaving total incomes, and any immediate reason for lower money demand, unchanged.

Furthermore, being nonproductive transfer income, interest at higher rates may encourage saving by those who receive them and discourage spending by those who pay them, but equally higher rates of interest discourage saving by those who pay them and encourage spending by those who receive them. Those who receive higher interest will both save and spend more because of higher incomes; those who pay higher interest will both save and spend less because of lower incomes. Any difference arising out of a changed situation will be minimal and not necessarily in any particular direction. Higher or lower rates of interest have no direct effect upon money demand or inflation.

Higher rates of interest do have a secondary, or consequent, effect on money demand, but with no effect whatsoever on inflation—only on employment. The transfer of income from profit to interest, and the attraction of funds from business use to government use by the payment of higher rates, necessarily mean that spending on replacement real capital from depreciation funds will be reduced. Reduced real capital in following periods means less labour employed, lower total wages, and lower production of goods and services. Reduced wage and total money incomes cause money demand to be lower, but only in proportion to productivity. Money demand relative to productivity remains the same, so prices and inflation cannot be affected. The value of real capital and share prices may suffer enormously in recessions caused by rates of interest being higher than rates of profit, but these have nothing to do with the prices of standard-of-living goods and services.

The Rate of Interest and International Trade

Unlike domestic exchanges of resources for produced goods and services, international exchanges are of imports for exports, each of which may be goods or services at any stage of processing. As far as exporters are concerned, they are final production.

So long as imports and exports have the same real value, each country gains from international trade. And, so long as the demand from abroad for our currency to buy our exports is the same as the supply to abroad of our currency used to purchase our imports, there is no interference with our monetary system. This can be achieved by equating the overseas demand for and supply of our currency (made available against trade documents only with allowances for tourism and travel) through rates of exchange.

Some imports and exports will not require payment and will consequently not enter into rates of exchange calculation. These are movements of items on capital, not current, account. That is, finance arrangements have been made with suppliers, or through third parties, that immediate payment is not required by the importing country. This presents absolutely no problem to either country.

In addition to international trade, there can be international finance of a country lending funds to another. Interest charges or profits remitted, being for goods and services received, would go into rates-of-exchange calculations. However, the transfer of funds on borrowing or repayment has nothing to do with real value and must not affect rates of exchange. Nor have they anything to do with rates of interest in the borrowing country. These are funds borrowed abroad at rates of interest available in that country and due for payment in that country's currency (hence the need for the interest to go into rates of exchange).

It is totally wrong in the first place to have rates of exchange that do not achieve a balance of payments for imports and exports on current account. For this, measurement of demand and supply for local currency, and control of rates of exchange, are necessary. Fixed rates of exchange are out, so are rates that dance up and down each hour; a monthly adjustment would probably suffice with reasonable data collection and statistical projection of likely trends. The system has never operated, so it is no good cynics saying that it has not worked in the past. The present "financial deregulation" or currency speculation system does not work either, as Australia can testify.

With a balance of payments on current account, there is no need to attract funds from abroad with high rates of interest to meet any shortfall. Even if there were a need to attract funds for any reason, high rates of interest is not the way to do it. Interest is paid on borrowed funds at rates of interest available in the lending country, not in the borrowing country. Understanding of international trade and finance went completely out when so-called financial deregulation came in. All that financial deregulation does is put international finance in the hands of currency speculators and lead countries into enormous foreign debts.

The Rate of Interest and the National Debt

Funds are owned, and owed, by people. The only uses for funds are by business (which may include on-lending to people at interest) and by government. Business use is on an equity (profit) or nonequity (interest) basis. Government use is for social purposes, which pays interest but has no revenue, so taxes on business activity are needed to finance the interest. Whether a government uses taxation or borrowed funds to finance a social project is simply a matter of whether it wants to pay for it out of taxes immediately or, plus interest, over a period of time.

There may be some justification in paying for a "capital" project over a period of time if that project will have social benefits for that time. However, as a government has many such projects every period, and the sinking-fund payments for past projects are likely to equal the capital payments for current projects, it would be much simpler, and less costly in total taxes, to pay for all projects out of current taxes. Applying business principles of capitalisation and period depreciation to social expenditure does not have the same logic, because the latter earns no future revenue to repay either the principal or the interest. This does not apply, of course, to government-owned businesses.

Nevertheless, governments have borrowed large sums at interest for nonbusiness use and built up enormous national debts, often with no future social benefits even for moral justification. Borrowing for war expenditure is an example—what future benefit is there in an exploded bomb? Interest on national debt of this nature results in a transfer of income from taxpayers to bondholders. This is totally unnecessary and could be removed at any time by purchasing outstanding interest-bearing certificates for noninterest-bearing certificates, i.e., cash.

One main reason why this conversion is not undertaken is that economists fear the resultant liquid position of people with cash—that they will rush out and buy goods and services, causing (more) inflation. This would be against all experience. People with cash, and loss of interest income, following the conversion would seek to recover income by competing for, or adding to, business investment. This would, no doubt, cause rates of interest and yields on equities to fall, but profits would rise and business activity would be stimulated to higher employment. A staged conversion may be needed to prevent a change that is too sudden.

This does not mean that governments cannot, or should not, borrow or have national debts in excess of their business funding. In fact, borrowing to increase, or liquidating part of, the national debt could be useful factors in rate of interest control to achieve its intended purpose of maintaining full employment. What the government offers as a rate of interest on borrowing is the only alternative to the business investment of funds, so this determines the minimum that business must offer and whether business investment is more favourable than the government rate of interest. Favourable business investment means a reinvestment of depreciation, and an inflow of other, funds for higher employment and production.

Cost Inflation and the Real Rate of Interest

It has already been established that wages set the real value of money for standard-of-living exchanges; money demand determines whether that real value is maintained for prices, and hence for depreciation, interest, and profits. Cost inflation exists when the cost of labour increases beyond that provided by productivity.

When cost inflation exists, funds lose real value, so lenders seek higher rates of interest to compensate for the loss in capital value of the funds lent. When the funds are returned, they will be worth less in real terms than when they were borrowed. The amount of extra interest required tends to equal the loss in capital value, so at 7 percent cost-inflation, rates of interest tend to rise by 7 percent.

The situation may be further complicated by the tax position of income in the hands of lenders. If dividends out of profits are tax-paid by the business but interest is not, then this is compared to the amount of interest after tax and after compensating for cost inflation. This further increases the amount of interest needed to be competitive with dividends. On the other hand, cost inflation increases the replacement cost of real capital, so historical and official rates of depreciation will be insufficient for new purchases. Part of declared profits must be set aside as additional depreciation if that business is to survive cost-inflation conditions.

The real rate of interest needs to take into account cost inflation and rates of tax. The real rate of profit on equity funds needs to take into account the need for the extra replacement cost of real capital. These conditions make it very hard for investors to choose between higher income, taxed with loss of capital, and lower income with nominal capital gain (which may be taxed if sold to obtain funds). It is no wonder the investment market is fraught with danger and malpractice and that borrowers for business and homes have to pay enormous prices for their enterprise.

A home buyer with a $100,000 mortgage pays $7000 p. a. extra interest when wage inflation is running at 7 percent. The best bargain available to such persons would be to have wages increase only with productivity and get rid of the interest loading. Of course, those renting are in the same boat—rents include interest costs. Economists and wage bargainers who promote the idea that wages should be adjusted to "inflation" as measured by a consumer price index do a great disservice to everyone, particularly the wage-earners they claim to represent.

Chapter 6
Demand

Barter or Real Demand

When barter is used to make exchanges, there is no problem of demand not being equal to supply, or supply not being equal to demand. Every exchange is both supply and demand of equal value; demand must be equal to supply, and supply must be equal to demand, or neither would exist. Which is precisely the reason for the use of money.

Money Demand

The purpose of money is to facilitate exchanges that would not otherwise exist, thereby increasing our economic standards of living. This it does remarkably well. The shortcoming of the use of money is that it separates demand from supply, with no guarantee that one will equal the other unless the problem is recognised and managed to that end.

In business economies, the use of money as a medium of exchange in standard of living transactions is but one use of funds. Economic activity consists entirely of the purchase of resources for money incomes and the sale of resultant production for prices. No attempt is made to measure the supply of resources and money incomes, and make these equal in real and money terms to resultant production and prices on a continuing basis.

To be sure, money prices determine money incomes because the remainder of prices after other incomes goes to profits. But all that this does is to adjust next period's supply to this period's demand. If demand has been less than that necessary to provide satisfactory profits for total business and maintain production, production will be less next period. This is the downswing or recession in a trade cycle. If demand has been enough to provide satisfactory profits, production will be maintained or increased. This is the upswing or recovery in a trade cycle. There is no mechanism by which demand is measured and controlled to supply so that, no matter what resources are used in production, there will be enough money demand for that production to provide satisfactory profits, and maintain or increase production.

Demand and Inflation

The level of money demand for business production establishes prices; it therefore determines whether the real value for money set by wages is maintained for the rest of the total business exchange. Changes in the rate of interest have been shown to have no immediate effect upon incomes and demand. However, rate changes relative to the average rate of profit of all business do have a consequent effect upon the level of business activity. They influence whether investment in real capital, and therefore employment and productivity, is maintained, increased, or decreased. When money demand changes in the same direction as productivity, there is no effect on prices and inflation.

For labour to accept control of total wages that precludes cost inflation or deflation, assurance will have to exist that demand inflation will not occur, raising prices and profits, and leaving real wages behind in following periods. Is this risk the price of achieving full employment?

The answer is that measurement and control of money demand to preclude demand inflation or deflation will be just as much a function of monetary management as is measurement and control of total wages. Control over total wages will set a real value for money wages; control over total demand will maintain it for prices, depreciation, interest, and profits. Whilst measurement of the level of unemployment will be a significant reference guide to raising or lowering the rate of interest to avoid over- or under-employment, further data will provide information on productivity, money demand, depreciation, interest, and profits.

Demand and the Rate of Interest

Any tendency for money demand to rise relative to productivity, or for average profits to rise above the rate of interest, will be a signal to raise interest rates to average rates of profit, and so defuse any movement towards demand inflation. It is not even necessary for average profits to exceed the rate of interest during the initial buildup from recession to full employment, because rate equality will provide for a gradual return to full employment. People are forever hopeful that their equity investment will provide better returns than the rate of interest. They will act on the guarantee that average profits will at least equal the rate of interest, no matter how many resources are used.

The rate of interest that ensures full employment establishes the demand conditions that maintain the real value for money for a production period. Coupled with control of total wages to avoid cost inflation, that real value can be maintained through time.

Money demand needs to be measured, and controlled via the rate of interest's effect on employment, because our use of funds as money leaves no other association between real supply and real demand. In a business economy, the real supply of resources used must come before the real demand for the goods and services produced from those resources. Money demand will come from spending out of resource incomes, plus any net spending of funds. This must raise total spending to about the level where profits average the rate of interest. Any trend away from this result requires rate of interest adjustment.

With no recognition of this vital point, and no management to achieve it, the amount of funds spent on demand for goods and services, in addition to the direct spending out of incomes, can, conceivably, be any figure at all.

There are banking regulations that impose some limits on credit creation through assets to equity and cash ratios, but these are arbitrary. Trade-cycle experience is that, with cost inflation, rates of interest are usually too high and money demand too low to provide for full employment. Demand deflation is the major problem, not demand inflation. Even so, measurement and control are necessary to ensure that neither too much, nor too little, money demand eventuates.

Chapter 7
Wages

Wages and the Real Value of Money

It has been established that labour is the only fundamental productive resource. However, in a period that must start with production saved from previous periods, that saving, called real capital, is coupled with labour as improved labour, in productivity.

It follows that, whilst the wages of labour is the fundamental cost of production, depreciation of real capital is a period cost of production, and, as a part of the cost of improved labour, a necessary part of total income. The use of funds to facilitate the bringing together of labour and real capital in production, their use as money to facilitate the exchanges of resources used for resultant production, and the use of our social environment cause interest, profit, and tax costs also to be transfers from the generative income of improved labour. Thus the total income of improved labour less the period or transfer incomes of depreciation, interest, profits, and taxes give the net period income of labour as wages.

Of total presale incomes, wages is the only one that is not a predetermined deduction or a transfer deduction from the cost of improved labour, so wages set the real value for money for presale incomes in a production period. It has been shown that the real value for money established by wages can be maintained for prices and postsale incomes by management of the rate of interest.

However, to obtain a continuation of that same real value for money for the next and future production periods, it is obvious that total wages must be measured and controlled relative to the new productivities. Total wages must not be allowed to forge ahead, or lag behind, the real value of money already established. Otherwise, transactions that overlap periods—recovery by depreciation of capital expenditure and profit incomes in particular—will not realise the real value that was expected of them. In fact, most transactions overlap production periods, because most production is continuous, not periodic. Changes in the real value of money mean that incomes earned, even wages, do not purchase the real value that was expected when the resources were used.

In many countries, workers place undue emphasis on increasing money wage rates rather than increasing real wages. Money wages can be increased to any figure that one likes to nominate, but this in itself will not increase real wages one iota. Wages rates of a million dollars a week or even a million dollars an hour can be paid, but with no more being produced, how can real wages increase? Compensating adjustments will be made to rates of interest, amounts of depreciation that must be recovered to replace real capital, prices and profits. There would be disastrous losses by those who are owed money, and equal gains by those who owe money—except that very high rates of interest would in time tend to smooth out some differences. Consequent unemployment, higher taxes, and pricing chaos would make for lower standards of living all round—just as happens on a lesser scale when wage rates are arbitrarily adjusted by any figure that causes cost inflation. There has never been any gain to wage earners from increasing wage rates on a national basis above the level proposed in this book. Any gain that accrues to some wage earners from having their rates increased must come at the expense of other wage earners.

Indexation of Total Wages

The problem of how to manage total wages so that the new real value for money that they set for the future will be the same as that for the present and the past can now be readily solved. It is known how to measure productivity from hours worked and real capital used, so the target for total prices can be calculated using a constant multiplier. Depreciation is known. The same (monthly) data collection from all businesses will give total equity and nonequity funds in use, interest income, and taxes payable. From these figures it can be seen and calculated that total wages must get all of the value of productivity at a constant real value for money except for depreciation, taxes, and total funds used times the rate of interest (profit on equity funds is to average the rate of interest).

Actual wage rates must, therefore, be indexed so that new wages rates cause total wages to receive all of this calculated figure. This indexation must apply to all wage rates from directors and chief executives to the lowest paid employees, and it must be used at a point in time (probably annually), after taking into account all other wage-rate determinations. If no other changes have been made to wage rates, this indexation will have the effect of increasing money wages with increases in productivity. Examples below show that real wages actually gain progressively, rather than proportionately, from the increases in productivity that arise through greater use of real capital—which fact has been brought out through time since the Industrial Revolution, and would have progressed much faster except for the repeated setbacks of trade-cycle conditions.

Indexation Methods

Although wages are defined as the cost of labour, the term *wages* includes much more than just the payments for hours worked that go into productivity. Wages includes all salaries, commissions, bonuses, holiday pay, annual leave, sick leave, long service leave, termination pay, workers compensation, retirement benefits, in fact all of the costs of labour. The total of these, divided by hours actually worked, gives the effective rate per hour worked.

It is the total costs of labour that have to be indexed on the basis of periodic calculation. This change in wages can be passed on in many different ways, and not necessarily in the same way to all employees. It may be used to provide superannuation benefits, additional holidays or leave, fewer hours worked for the same weekly pay, or higher rates per hour worked.

Generally the adjustments will be relatively small (e.g., about 2 percent per annum) and may tend to be taken in higher rates per hour worked. However, they provide a painless way towards shorter working weeks, which have long been a feature of progress in standards of living (although not necessarily at the time they became operative). A move from 40 hours to 39 hours with no change in weekly pay represents an increase in wage rates of two and a half percent. A number of smaller reductions in hours per week worked is much to be preferred over massive reductions like 40 hours to 36, which nominally reduces production and standards of living by 10 percent, but in effect calls for more overtime at higher rates of pay. An increase in paid annual leave from, say, three weeks to four effectively increases wage rates per hour worked by more than 2 percent. People have differing requirements for their standards of living, and to the extent that businesses can accommodate them, they should have the opportunity to express their individual or group choices.

Where other increases in wage rates have taken total wages above the required figure, and a reduction is required by indexation, there will be little choice but to reduce all hourly wage rates as the means of avoiding cost inflation. This does not reduce real wages, just as increasing money wage rates above monetary management indexation does not increase real wages.

Some countries, like Australia, make disastrous legal judgments on many wage rates, increasing them by faulty logic on changes in a Consumer Price Index (which is said to represent the level of inflation). Monetary management indexation should replace this procedure. No consumer price index can ever represent controllable inflation, because prices are subject to the vagaries of uncontrollable nature. The index contains only a selection of prices, including some that should not be there as they are affected by imports. In any case, increasing wages because of the cost inflation of wage rises is just absurd—all that it does is to perpetuate inflation.

Chapter 8
International Trade and Finance

General

The total business exchange of resources used for resultant production through the medium of money provides economic standards of living. Some of resultant production can be used to further increase satisfaction by exchanging this for commodities either not produced locally or produced more cheaply overseas. Differences between countries in the availability of nature's materials and services, like minerals and climate, account for much of the reason for international trade, though production volumes and people skills are also very significant factors.

There are three distinct aspects of international trade that must be considered separately to reach the understanding that provides for its proper management. Otherwise, monetary problems, such as imbalances of trade on current account and mounting international debts, occur. The three aspects are the trading of exports for imports to improve standard of living satisfactions for both exporters and importers, the import of real capital on a delayed-payment basis by countries to improve their productivities, and the transfer of funds between countries to facilitate production when funds may not be available locally for specific ventures.

Current Account Trading

This is nearer to barter than business activity in that goods and services are traded for goods and services, not resources used for resultant production. But trading is still conducted through the medium of money, and the use of money in these trades must be properly managed. Interest and taxes payable abroad must, of course, be included in the current account. Exports earn foreign currency, but exporters want local funds, so there is a demand in foreign currency for local funds. Imports require foreign currency to pay for them, so there is a supply of local funds to purchase foreign currency. The demand for and supply of local funds, and the matching supply of and demand for foreign currencies, must be measured and rates of exchange established so that each supply and demand is made equal.

Of course, not every country that exports to is going to import from another particular country, at least, not to comparable levels of real value for which satisfactory rates of exchange may be established. Where this happens, instead of offering one's own funds to another country to pay for imports, the surplus funds from exports to another country may be offered. This becomes rather complex, and unfortunately is mostly resolved by dealing through the funds of major countries, like United States dollars and Japanese yen. Computer facilities could deal with such complex calculations, and an international rates of exchange calculation bureau could process the data to provide every country with weekly or monthly rate results for use until the next calculation.

With only imports that have to be paid for, and exports that are paying for them, going into such calculations, they would be subject to seasonal fluctuations, such as the export of the Australian wheat and wool. Statistical handling of forecasts and projections up to a year ahead could largely smooth out these seasonal fluctuations. However, such a bureau does not exist, and each country meanwhile will have to do its best on its own account, buying and selling some other currencies to best advantage to offset some import and export surpluses. Results in any case will be better than the crazy speculation, called financial deregulation, that is practised now.

Financial deregulation of international trade means that all currencies are put on the market for anyone to buy and sell, and thus establish rates of exchange. Because trading is not limited to those importers and exporters of goods and services, and is open to speculators, these rates of exchange cause large discrepancies to occur between the values of imports and exports. Such discrepancies are said to be compensated for by large flows of funds between countries—funds that have to be attracted by offering artificially high rates of interest. Of course, where exchange rates are out of line and discrepancies persist, huge international debts build up. International currency speculators have a bonanza playing the market at the expense not only of international traders, like farmers and graziers, but of all who see their heritages invaded by foreign ownership.

However, another way of looking at this financial deregulation problem is that countries that offer high rates of interest attract foreign investment funds, which creates a demand for their currency. This demand increases the price of, say, Australian dollars, making Australian exports more expensive in foreign currencies and harder to sell. It also reduces the prices of foreign currencies, making imports cheaper to buy in Australia. Both react to cause Australia to have enormous balance-of-payments problems and mounting foreign debts. The apparent solution under financial deregulation of high rates of interest to Australia's international trade problem, is in fact the cause of the problem!

When real imports are matched to real exports through controlled rates of exchange to achieve a balance of payments on current account, there is no change to the real value of the total resultant production of an economy and no change to total money prices or incomes. Any other situation results in problems.

Capital Account Financing

Developed countries often find themselves in a position of being able to export goods and services to developing countries on the basis of receiving import payments in later periods. This is very similar to domestic situations of using current resources to produce goods that provide no immediate benefit but provide more benefits through their use later on.

Exports on capital account that do not have to be paid for out of this period's imports do not enter into rates of exchange calculations. Instead the debt remains in the books of lenders and borrowers to be serviced through trading account payments for interest and capital via imports at arranged times.

No flow of funds between countries is involved. Borrowing countries have book debts owing to lending countries in terms of the currencies of the lending countries. These simply sit there, earning arranged interest, until trading account imports pay off the interest and capital.

Transfers of Funds

One reason for transferring funds to another country is to facilitate business ventures that cannot arrange satisfactory local funding. These funds may be required for local purchases and must therefore be converted to local currency. Banks will exchange foreign currency for local currency and take over ownership of the former, or lend local currency against the holding of foreign funds. These, and any types of fund transfers between countries, can take place at whatever rates of exchange the participants agree upon (and they will probably be based on established current account trading rates), but whatever happens, they must not affect the calculation of trading rates of exchange.

The inflow of funds, giving rise to more money demand, mentioned in the previous paragraph, is no different in effect from credit creation by a bank. If demand increases to the stage where it tends to inflate prices and profits rather than increase production in the same ratio, this will show up, and local rates of interest will be increased to offset the trend. However, as explained earlier, rarely is extra money demand inflationary; it is usually wage rates that cause cost inflation, and lack of money demand that causes unemployment.

International Money

Having an international currency would be an advanced way of simplifying many problems of international trade and travel. Instead of having a multitude of rates of exchange, each country would have one rate of exchange only—between its money unit and the international money unit. Every participating country would accept international currency for its exports and pay for its imports in the same way. Travellers would be able to purchase goods and services with one international currency wherever they were and readily be able to compare prices without having to make numerous exchange rate calculations. A self-financing international bureau would establish all (monthly) rates of exchange into international currency, buying and selling individual currencies, probably dealing as wholesalers with banks only, at a very small service charge. Noncurrent account movements of funds would not be included. The United Nations could well sponsor such a venture.

Chapter 9
Monetary Management

The Factors

Three factors have been identified as being necessary to measure and control if the use of money is not to cause inflation, unemployment or trade imbalances. These are wage indexation to obviate any tendency to cost inflation or deflation through time, rate-of-interest control to maintain full employment and obviate any tendency to demand inflation or deflation, and rates-of-exchange control to achieve a balance of payment on current account in international trade. No other measure is necessary.

Governments may have any budget policy of taxation and expenditure that they wish. The ownership of existing things may pass between people and governments. Funds may flow between countries. Prices of individual commodities may change with tastes and market demand. Wage rates may move with the business demand for labour types needed to meet that market demand. No amount of dynamic movement in any of these areas has any effect whatsoever, provided control is established and maintained by monetary management procedures. These basically maintain money at a constant real value through time for incomes and prices. Total money flows only are affected. Individual incomes and prices keep their relativities as established by market forces of supply and demand. Production and exchanges operate as they should operate, with demand always equal to the current level of supply and money maintained at a constant real value.

The Mechanism

The administration of national wage indexation, rates of interest, and rates of exchange is purely a statistical exercise of data collection and processing. The wage indexes issued by the monetary management authority will be legally enforceable to have that effect; interest rates will be managed through Treasury borrowing and trading; rates of exchange will be issued monthly. Administrators of monetary management must be free from political control or influence once enabling legislation is passed.

It is proposed that all businesses will be registered and that each will be required to submit a monthly return for monetary management purposes. Businesses include every organisation with sales (probably in excess of twenty-five thousand dollars per annum), from sole proprietors with no employees (professions, trades, shopkeepers, etc.) to the largest corporations and public utilities. A sample of businesses may also be asked to submit data on a weekly basis to give earlier indications of trends that may be developing. Much data is already collected by the Australian Bureau of Statistics; this could probably be respecified and the same avenue used.

Each return would show for this period Sales Revenue, Purchases from Other Businesses, Wages, Interest Payable to People, Taxes, Depreciation, Profit, Hours Worked, Interest-bearing Debt, Equity, and Assets. Forecast figures for the next period would also be requested. Sales would include sales taxes and any interest receivable. Purchases would include interest payable to other businesses, such as banks. Wages would be gross, including tax and deductions payable to others on behalf of wage earners.

Taxes would exclude tax on wages but include payroll, sales and private taxes. Sales less Purchases, Wages, Interest, Taxes, and Depreciation will equal Profit from trading. Depreciation and profit may not be the same figures used to calculate company income-tax payable, but are the ones that can be used by each business to assess its economic viability. Monetary management will, of course, use national totals only; individual returns will be confidential.

The first thing to be determined is whether Wage Rates need to be indexed to maintain a constant ratio between Productivity and Final Sales (i.e., making sure that there is no cost inflation or deflation between periods). Productivity will be calculated by multiplying totals of Hours Worked times Assets Value. Required Final Sales will be calculated by multiplying Productivity by its established Constant. This will be compared to actual Final Sales, being the totals of Sales Revenue less Purchases from Other Businesses. If current and next-period forecast figures show a significant trend in Actual Final Sales away from Required Final Sales, Total Wages will need to be adjusted via Wage Rate Indexation to bring them into line.

The effective Rate of Interest calculated from totals of Interest Payable to People and Interest-Bearing Debt will be compared to the effective Rate of Profit, which is calculated from totals of Equity and Profits. If there is a tendency for the rates to diverge, action will be needed to adjust the rates of interest offered on government borrowing to bring the rates back into line. This action will be taken into consideration along with information of levels of Unemployment, which, seasonally adjusted, should stay fairly steady at something under two percent. A rise in unemployment would confirm the need to lower rates of interest. Adjustments at any one time would be small fractions of a percentage point.

Rates of Exchange calculation will be a completely separate exercise. Businesses requiring foreign currencies will lodge supporting documents for the real imports involved; those providing foreign currencies will lodge supporting documents for the real exports involved. In and out tourist requirements will be added. Calculations made at existing rates of exchange will determine whether a net deficit or surplus of Australian currency results. Where there is a trend towards increasing deficits or surpluses, changes in rates of exchange will be required. The particular rates to change will depend upon differences arising between the supply and demand for those currencies, subject of course to forward projections that are made and probably taking into consideration the changes in wage rates of some countries. Where there is a tendency to cost inflation, that country's currency is likely to be devalued. New rates of exchange will be issued monthly where changes are necessary.

Stocks

It could be assumed, without too much inaccuracy for monetary management purposes, that stocks brought forward from last period equalled stocks carried forward to the next period. Stocks include raw materials, work in progress, and finished goods, i.e., anything not finally sold that has had labour expended on it. When monetary management is in operation, this will be more true than it currently is.

In trade-cycle conditions, stocks do tend to rise and fall significantly, and perhaps should be taken into account in initial data gathering and calculations. In times of recession, stocks rise because of the lag in restricting production to lower levels of demand. In times of recovery, stocks fall because businesses are anxious to quit excess stocks and to avoid the overstocked situation that they have just been through.

Brought forward stocks show up as real capital in its broad sense of owned things existing at the start of a period. Depreciation is 100 percent when stocks are used, unlike things that provide repeated services to production over a number of periods until worn out or replaced.

Chapter 10
Outline Examples

Productivity Example

Say a model economy practising monetary management works 2 million hours in a year and uses $200 million of real capital. An amount of $125 million is equity funded and $125 million is funded at the rate of interest. By using the short-term formula of annual hours worked/1000 times real capital/100,000, productivity is calculated at 4 million units. The constant used to maintain the real value of money is $7.50 per productivity unit. This values expected production at $30 million. The current rate of interest is 4 percent p.a., and average capital depreciates over twenty years.

Final sales of resultant production reach the target of $30 million. Wages receive $10 million, interest paid is $5 million, depreciation requires $10 million, leaving $5 million profit. Gross national income is $30 million; net national income is $20 million—half to labour and half to capital. Real capital is maintained at $200 million by the spending of depreciation funds of $10 million on replacement buildings and plants.

It is at least as rewarding to spend depreciation funds on replacement assets as it is to retire interest-bearing debt or invest elsewhere at the rate of interest. It is also more likely that this course will be taken because of commitments that would increase costs per unit if levels of production were lowered by not replacing assets. Also, any significant move of funds from equity to interest-bearing investment is likely to reduce the rate of interest and so make that avenue even less attractive.

A continuation of full employment is assured, no matter what changes take place in the production, prices, and profits of individual businesses. Any effect of nature on resultant production is absorbed, because business profits are maintained regardless of whether good seasons force commodity prices down or bad seasons force prices up. Next year's effect of nature will be different, and that will be absorbed too. Business continuity depends upon monetary results, not real results. Real incomes are what we get after the effects of nature; whilst money incomes are assured, money cannot guarantee any real result.

Business Example

Say our economic model consists of a few businesses—A, B, and C. The number of businesses, sizes of figures, and the units used are of no significance. Figures used are in millions of dollars and millions of units. (See figure 1.)

The real units and funds employed may have been as in figure 2.

Total economic standards of living are provided by applying the productivity of 2 million units of labour and $200 million real capital (calculated in a previous example as 4 million units) to nature, resulting in production that sells for $30 million. The $14 million of Purchases and $14 million of Intermediate Sales, of course, cancel out.

If the same total hours worked and real capital were used next period, the only way that cost inflation or deflation would not occur would be for total wages to remain at $10 million. The only way that demand inflation or deflation would not occur

Business	Wages	Interest	Purchases	Intermediate Sales	Final Sales	Depreciation	Profit
A	1	1	2	3	5	2	2
B	2	1	4	9	1	2	1
C	7	3	8	2	24	6	2
Totals	10	5	14	14	30	10	5

Figure 1

Business	Hours Worked	Real Capital	Non-Equity Funds	Equity Funds
A	0.2	60	25	50
B	0.4	40	25	25
C	1.4	100	75	50
Totals	2.0	200	125	125

Figure 2

would be for final sales to remain at \$30 million, in which case, with depreciation predetermined at \$10 million, interest and profit would get \$10 million between them—with virtually no reason to change their proportions.

However, should the rate of interest be raised (and this can be done by government direction), the complementary amount of total profit will fall. This will cause the amount of reinvestment in real capital to fall next period, employment and production will fall, and living standards will suffer. Such is the importance of measurement and control of rates of interest relative to rates of profit that, even though there is no cost or demand inflation or deflation, recessions will occur when interest rates exceed profit rates.

Recessions get worse when there is wage inflation and demand deflation, which are the conditions that many economies have suffered recently. Economists will all say that we have been suffering from too much demand, but only because they do not divide the problem into its two basic parts. They believe that to attack demand and inflation, high rates of interest must be used to cause business failures and unemployment. The high rates do achieve unemployment, but because they also reduce production in the same proportion, they do not have any effect on inflation. What a tragedy of ignorance!

A study of the example figures will show that, under monetary management, individual figures may change for wage rates, prices, profits, products, and number of businesses in any way that can be imagined, but, so long as totals are achieved, the monetary system works as it should. And it stays that way even if employment or real capital is increased, provided total wages are increased according to the indexation formula and total prices meet the new productivity times the constant. The economy can be as dynamic as people and nature like to make it, and monetary management will still cope.

Model Changes

All manner of changes may be considered to see their effects via the economic model.

Say that next period investment in real capital and funding are increased by 1 percent to $202 million and $252.5 million respectively, and used with the same labour. This increases productivity to 4.04 million units. At the constant $7.50 per unit, final sales are targetted at $30.3 million. Interest on $126.5 million amounts to $5.05 million, depreciation is $10.1 million, profit requires $5.05 million, so wages must be indexed to receive $10.1 million. This represents a rise in real and money wages of 1 percent for no change in total hours worked.

Labour shares in productivity that is increased through more real capital without itself having to make any further contribution. This has been the basis for the increased standards of living for all since the Industrial Revolution. Steady and greater progress has been marred only by the lack of monetary management and resultant trade cycles.

Should the rate of interest fall to say 3.96 percent, interest and profit on $250 million funds would amount to $19.9 million, requiring $10.1 million to go to wages—a rise of 1 percent in real and money wages for no change in labour input. When living standards increase through greater productivity, the ratio of consumption to production tends to fall, further increasing real capital and productivity. The funding for business activity tends to be more plentiful and cheaper; hours of work become less plentiful and relatively more expensive. The rate of interest and profit requirement on funds becomes less through time. Again labour gains without increasing its contribution.

Better quality labour in the original example may be used with the same hours worked and real capital to cause productivity to rise by 1 percent to 4.04 million units. Final sales will be $30.3 million. Funding is unchanged with interest and profit at $5 million each and depreciation is $10 million, so wages must be increased to $10.3 million. This is a rise of 3 percent in real and money wages for a rise of 1 percent in the quality of labour. Capital interests are no worse off, because prices and their incomes have not changed. There is no reason to change the level of activity and employment. Labour's share of the national income rises from 50 percent to nearly 53 percent. More skilled labour and better work practices have this effect—fewer working hours and production-restricting work practices offset it.

When labour income is twice capital income, which is nearer to reality than the model, a rise of 1 percent in productivity through better quality labour or real capital gives labour a gain of 1.5 percent in real and money wages. That is, $0.3 million rise on $20 million wages, rather than $0.3 million on $10 million. Still a very handsome reward for no change in hours worked.

Chapter 11
Employment

Hours of Work

Discussion has so far centred on whether a person is employed or unemployed, but this distinction is very crude. It is acceptable only for trade-cycle conditions where unemployment ranges up to ten percent and more. In addition to the unemployed, there are always many employed people who are either underemployed or overemployed so far as their individual preferences are concerned. This means that if their choices could be met, they would work more hours or fewer hours. Their standards of living and qualities of life would be improved if they could work longer hours and earn more, or work fewer hours and earn less. People are individuals and are only best satisfied when their individual preferences are met as closely as is possible.

Not all choices can be met with employment opportunities to the extent that they can just balance their needs between leisure and the real wages of employment. But the principle needs to be recognised, and the myth exploded, that fewer hours necessarily represent better conditions. The more people who can come closer to their balance between work and leisure, the better will be their standard of living.

There is no reason why one person's choice should affect the quality of life of any other person—within the limits of common sense and community acceptance, of course. No one wants to see a person voluntarily working such long hours that safety or health is compromised. Every reasonable exchange transaction means an addition to someone's standard of living. There is never any suggestion that one person in work takes the job of another, or that an older person should retire to make way for someone younger. This is nonsense where demand is always matched to supply by monetary management. If both are employed, money demand will match their total output.

Industrialised nations have gone through periods of successive reductions in "standard" hours worked—48 to 44, to 40, and now to 36 or 35. Each adjustment has been claimed as a victory for workers over their employers, when in fact more workers may have lost in living standards than the number who gained. Many would have preferred to retain their real wages rather than see them reduced by higher prices and underemployment. Some may have been able to retain their real wages by working more than the new standard hours to meet the higher prices. Some, no doubt, were satisfied to work shorter weeks for the same money wages and pay the higher prices. All would have been disillusioned to some extent, because reduced hours were claimed because of productivity increases that would not result in higher prices. The increased productivity would have already reduced prices, so a subsequent change to higher labour costs per hour worked must increase them. Of course, there must be a long-term change to fewer hours worked as productivity per head of population increases and the satisfaction from more goods and services gives way to satisfaction from more leisure.

Just as employers can (apart from existing legal restrictions) offer any wage rate, so can they offer any hours of work. The adjustments at any one time to working hours on offer should be small, so as not to disrupt existing conditions too much—and not all employees will want to change. If significant underemployment results, many workers will be worse off through less production and higher prices. Employers do not grant shorter standard working weeks—employees bring them on themselves, for better or worse. Some expect to gain, and may do so, through penalty rates for overtime worked.

Adjustments of four or more hours at a time in standard working weeks are just too drastic in their effects. Any adjustment in hours worked per week, even of a few minutes, must have a proportionate adjustment in weekly wage rates so that they provide the same rate per hour worked. Otherwise, such adjustment amounts to a wage-rate increase, which will be cost inflationary unless there is overall wage indexation. A tradeoff of less time worked or a wage-rate increase has already been discussed under the Wage Indexation of national monetary management.

The notion of a national standard working week could well be abandoned in favour of each business, or section of a business, offering hours of work that best suit the business and the majority of employees. Agreed hours will tend to be the current standard in many cases, but other businesses might offer fewer or more hours at competitive hourly rates of pay. These hours may either suit the majority of employees or attract the number of employees required for this type of employment. Workers will tend to move to businesses that offer the number of hours of work and rates of pay that suit them as individuals. Penalty rates for overtime would apply only when hours worked exceed agreed standards for the business.

Of course, any payment for time not worked, such as holidays, leave, workers compensation payments, etc., effectively increases wage rates per hour worked. Any increase in such payments, therefore, amounts to an increase in wage rates and must be taken into account in national Wage Indexation procedures.

Labour Productivity

Labour today has virtually no productivity of its own and is only employably productive when it is used with real capital. Labour productivity really means the productivity of labour using current real capital. But there is no doubt that there are many instances where labour productivity can be increased through better work practices without further increasing real capital or worsening conditions of employment.

Employees who impose production limitations through dargs or working to regulations, when they could produce more in the same time for no real loss of conditions, foolishly reduce their own and everyone else's standards of living. This situation mostly arises out of employee distrust of our trade cyclic economic system in the belief that the employer is the one who suffers the losses and that the extra labour required for production keeps themselves and mates in jobs. There will be no basis for such distrust to exist in the full employment and automatic wage indexation of national monetary management.

Simple examples given in Chapter 10 show that most of the benefits from more productive work practices accrue to wage earners.

Australian Wages System

To break the Australian wages system out of its cycle of increases for some sections that mean disadvantage to other sections, and so on, together with overall "cost of living" increases for most sections, will take a little time and understanding. Of course, monetary management indexation will immediately prevent future cost inflation, but it will preserve rather than fix any anomalies between rates for various occupations.

The function of any centralised or other legal wage determinations need not change, except to recognise that an indexation will be superimposed on all wage and salary rates, whether award or not. This will not change their relativity to each other, only preserve the real value of the money unit used. Legal wage determination should then be interested only in wage relativities and areas of unemployment to correct anomalies.

Where a trade or an industry is suffering unemployment, which may be due to high wage rates relative to other trades or industries, consideration may be given to reducing wage rates both to discourage entering those occupations and to encourage higher employment. Such reductions would automatically increase wage rates in all areas at the next wage indexation. Of course, where wage rates are below those for comparable occupations and there is no sectional unemployment, increases may be granted. If these are relatively few, they may be absorbed by increased productivity and so not mean any all round reduction at the next indexation.

Although adjustment is always a continuing process, most wage rates would tend to settle down and get their only increases through indexation when increased productivity makes these possible. In the past, productivity increases have averaged about two percent per annum, but significant increases could be expected by the monetary management removal of conflict between labour and capital interests.

Chapter 12
Saving

Real or Money Saving?

Politicians and economists frequently exhort the community to save more, as if saving were a virtue. Their reasoning is that saving is necessary both to reduce the money demand that causes inflation and to provide the funds for investment in real capital that will maintain our living standards. They happen to be wrong on both counts.

It has already been shown that wage increases beyond proposed monetary management levels are the cause of cost inflation and that demand deflation is practised to try to offset this. Also that rates of interest, increased by the level of cost inflation, are usually in excess of the average rate of profit of total business, so that funds are channelled away from investment in real capital and unemployment increases. Living standards are not maintained, especially for the unemployed, those who are on fixed incomes, and those who have saved. We are exhorted to cut our own throats by saving!

There is obviously no link in the present use of money between the saving of money and investment in real capital. An act of saving does not necessarily result in an act of investment; for economists to say that they are equal is only a confusion of terms. Real assets, or investment, is every owned thing that exists at the start of a period—i.e., saved from previous periods. This real saving has nothing to do with money, which cannot be saved, or funds, whose total is zero.

Money saved out of incomes, including the recovery of capital expenditure through depreciation, goes into the pool of funds. What comes out of that pool to be spent on consumption and real capital is completely independent of the addition to, or the total of, saved funds. Whether current spending from funds is more or less than current saving into funds depends mainly upon the relationship between the real rate of interest and the average rate of profit, because reinvestment in real and working capital is the major part of this spending.

Because the distinction between funds (used to facilitate production) and money (the medium of exchange) has been made, it can be said that a community cannot save money. Any person, and indeed every person, can save some money income, so long as that total saving is totally spent in another way, e.g., by the finance organisations that receive the savings. Otherwise money is not being used as a medium of exchange. Although the saved money income will probably merge into the pool of bank deposit funds (it could go under mattresses), this loss as a medium of exchange can be compensated for by spending funds as money on goods and services, provided the spending happens in the same period as the saving.

The problem of saving in some periods and spending in others is that there is a breakdown in the use of money as a medium of exchange in each period. Too little spending in the saving periods will result in demand deflation; additional spending in later periods will result in demand inflation. This may, or may not, be partially offset by carry-over stocks of unsold production from the periods of saving to the periods of spending—certainly there is no measurement or monetary management control to ensure that spending is at the required level.

Total spending of the required amount to match demand to

any level of supply in a managed monetary system does not differentiate between consumption and investment spending. So long as total spending is sufficient, investment spending will be sufficient, whether that spending comes from present saving of incomes, past accumulation of funds, or new generation of funds. This is so because investment spending on real capital is not made for its own sake, but to make things that will help to produce more goods and services for consumption. Consumption production is the only production to increase standards of living, but of course investment production is required to maintain future production for consumption.

By exhorting people to save in an unmanaged monetary system, consumption spending is decreased, making those businesses less profitable. They will require less replacement of real capital, making that production less profitable. Saving defeats the purpose of having funds spent on investment. It would be better by far to encourage consumer spending to improve profits and so cause spending on real capital to increase. Increases in rates of interest "to encourage saving" have the effect of reducing profits and reducing investment spending.

Superannuation and Welfare Pensions

One of means of saving proposed by politicians is that everyone should invest in superannuation schemes to provide funds for their retirement so that they will not become burdens on society. Tax concessions on contributions encourage this.

As explained earlier about saving, anyone can save money, which probably goes into funds, so long as an equal amount is spent from funds. This saving can be spent later on, so long as there is other saving at the same time. If the whole community both saves money and spends from funds at the same time, the pluses and minuses cancel out to no net effect.

The real situation is that people now working must produce enough to share with those who are retired, and when present workers retire, the people then working must produce enough to share with them. Superannuation funds will only provide goods and services for the retired, if the money saving involved causes real investment to be increased, and future labour becomes that much more productive than it would otherwise have been.

If spending is diverted from consumption by superannuation saving, that production becomes less profitable and the demand for investment production falls off. This defeats the whole purpose of superannuation. It is spending on consumption that promotes spending on investment. Investment spending will only proceed at the pace that people want in order to maintain consumption. The rate of real investment cannot be increased by government edict or inducement to save.

Providing for retirement requires an ongoing transfer of purchasing power via taxes on business transactions. When an economy is operating at full employment, living standards are maximised within the environment, which includes taxes. More cannot be produced just by saying that saving should be increased and that this will result in investment production. Money saving through superannuation schemes requires expensive administration and wastes resources. Logically, superannuation at the general level should be replaced by an unfunded national pension scheme financed directly out of taxation.

Chapter 13
Government Budget

The Revenue Budget

The government budget of revenue and expenditure is not meant to be a tool of economic or monetary management. Its purpose is to collect taxes as efficiently as possible on a socially accepted basis, and to provide these funds for required social administration and welfare. There should be no intended deficit or surplus of significant size, as this indicates a lack of management in undertaking the task.

Of course, the economic functions often associated with budget deficit or surplus manipulation of an economy are not needed when monetary management procedures are operating. There is no need to subsidise some businesses just to increase activity; this is unfair to those paying the extra tax. However, if the government wishes to subsidise some industry for general social reasons, like the local production of defence equipment, that is a different matter and an acceptable tax burden. There is no need to encourage saving by exempting some parts of income from tax; again this is wrong in principle and unfair in practice.

Taxation Methods

Present methods of taxation leave a lot to be desired. They are mostly based on personal incomes and business profits, the determination of which is so complex that tax law is both a nightmare for the conscientious and a haven for those who endeavor to shirk their share. In addition there are taxes on wholesale sales, payrolls, capital gains, land holdings, stamp duties on transactions, fringe benefits, etc. Many of the supplementary taxes are levied on earnings that have already paid income tax. The bureaucracy to collect the complete range of taxes is enormous, inefficient, and wasteful. Taxes have grown and multiplied as the needs have arisen. Rarely is there any downward adjustment, for (as Parkinson would say) expenditure will always increase to absorb the revenue raised. The insidious bracket creep of tax on inflationary wages increases the amount of tax collected at higher rates, reducing real wages in the process.

With the majority of tax levied on personal incomes and business profits, the effect is that those who contribute most to our standards of living are the ones who pay the most tax. It would seem to be more logical for those who take most from the pool of goods and services to pay the most tax. Taxes should be levied on the ones who benefit, not the ones who provide the benefits.

Of course, there is a significant correlation between those who earn more and those who consume more, because income earners have the funds and the capacity to purchase. But there are many exceptions. Some who provide valuable resources, and therefore earn a lot, live very simply—should they pay a lot of tax or a little? There are many who spend heavily on credit, taking more from the pool than they contribute—would it not be fairer that they pay taxes at the time of spending, rather than later when (and if) they earn enough to make repayments?

But the most important factor in favour of a tax related to consumption rather than production is that it can be collected from relatively few businesses instead of from every person and business. And it could be done as one simple tax, not as a multitude of different and complex taxes. Most of the same data that is required for monetary management could be used for progressive tax collection from businesses only on a monthly basis.

For example, if tax were payable on net business sales only—no personal income, business profits or other taxes. Each business is required to submit its sales figures. Tax would be payable monthly on sales less purchases (including purchases of assets) from other registered businesses. These purchases would have to be itemised by identified and eligible suppliers to claim a deduction. Some businesses would not be eligible suppliers (except by special arrangements to particular businesses)—e.g., retail food shops—because their sales are purely for consumption, not for incorporation into later consumer goods. Businesses would not fail to register, because their sales to other businesses would not be deductible, and they would not be able to get audit certificates for their accounts. Purchases that are listed by eligible supplier would be accumulated nationwide from all returns to check that those suppliers declared similar amounts as their sales. This, together with audit responsibilities to ensure that all sales were properly declared, would make tax reporting almost completely proof from evasion and avoidance.

The inclusion of asset purchases in the deduction from sales means that new or expanding businesses would not pay tax until capital costs had been offset by sales. Of course, there is then no deduction for depreciation. This is probably a fairer method of assessing tax—many a new business has failed having paid company tax in its early years without ever fully depreciating its capital expenditure.

Consumption taxes that collect amounts on individual transactions, like adding x percent to the shop price on each sales docket, are so inefficient in operation that they must have arisen out of someone's nightmare. They should be avoided at all costs. The price on an item must be the price payable, and tax must be payable not by the buyer, but by the seller on the monthly total net sales. Of course, sellers must pitch their prices to cover net-sales tax, which is a form of value-added tax, just as they now pitch their prices to cover company profit and other taxes. The incidence of the tax would fall most heavily on those who consume most of production, as distinct from personal income tax, which falls most heavily on those who contribute most to production.

It is suggested that the only businesses not required to pay net-sales tax would be those that sell or rent residential properties and accommodation. This would give a base of tax-free expenditure to everyone, and would make the rest of the tax progressive (i.e., the rich paying proportionately more) because accommodation forms a smaller proportion of higher spenders. The exemption would mean that people who rent accommodation would not be classed as businesses for tax purposes, which reduces the number of returns considerably, and from a social standpoint encourages investment in housing.

A further step to make the tax more progressive would require all businesses selling "luxuries" (e.g., jewellery, yachts) to pay a higher rate of tax, and "undesirables" (e.g., tobacco, alcohol) a higher rate still.

Export sales could, if desired, pay no, or less, tax. Imports would not qualify for deductions as purchases, making customs duty unnecessary—and clearing the way for better inspection against prohibited imports.

Any argument that a tax based on consumption rather than on income must be regressive (i.e., the poor pay proportionately more) is obviously nonsense. All social requirements can be built in without unduly complicating administration, which cannot be achieved with the present tax structure.

Chapter 14
Conclusion

The Big Picture

It is critical to economic understanding that business activity is recognised as total economic activity and that the level of business activity—i.e., total employment of resources and production of our economic standards of living—is determined by the relative returns on equity and non-equity funds invested.

There are only six types of resource used: nature, labour, real capital, social environment, equity funds, and non-equity funds—of which nature may be disregarded, except for social considerations, because its availability does not require the use of funds. Of the remaining resources, only two, labour and real capital in combination, are capable of production. Resultant production from the application of that productivity to, or within, nature is affected beyond human control by the vagaries of nature. Our social environment of laws and conventions allows business activity to take place as the production and exchange mechanism, and provides the recognition of funds to facilitate this. The use of funds, a creation of equal debits and credits, facilitates the bringing together of resources in production; some funds are used as money to act as the medium of exchange of resources used for resultant production. All resources require money income payments for their use.

There are only two types of resultant production—goods and services—but their sub-types are, of course, legion.

Because of the way that the business system operates, total money paid as incomes to resources is always just equal to total prices paid for goods and services sold. The business system pays wages for labour, thereby establishing the real value of money, sells production for prices, then pays taxes, interest, depreciation, and finally profits out of sales revenue.

Unless money is maintained at a constant real value through time, this apparent equality is not sufficient for money to act as a medium of exchange. In any one production period, money paid for some resources may not have the same real value per unit as money later paid for prices and other resources. Over time, the real value of money established by wage rates may not be the same as for previous periods.

Both of these changes to the real value of money have drastic repercussions on the continuity of business activity. Unless they are overcome by management of our monetary system, losses and gains in the real value of money interfere with the facilitation processes of funds and cause changes in resource usage, production, and standards of living.

When interest income is more rewarding than profit income, equity funds, particularly those available from depreciation recoveries, will not be spent on replacing real capital, but will be used to repay interest-bearing debt. This reduces total real capital, employment, and production.

When profit income is more rewarding than interest income, non-equity funds will flow to business use, expanding real capital, employment, and production.

Businesses constantly have funds (mainly from depreciation) available for reinvestment, and it is the decisions made on this reinvestment that determine whether trade-cycle recessions, recoveries, or neither ensue.

When it is equally rewarding to total business to reinvest

available funds either at the rate of interest or in real capital, there is no net incentive to repay debt. The continuation of business activity at its present level is, for the majority of business, the easiest and least risky way to go. It also offers the only chance to improve rewards, and equity providers are forever hopeful of this.

Of course, some business will be less than satisfactorily profitable and will prefer to reduce employment. Other business will be more than satisfactorily profitable and will prefer to increase employment. Together with the majority of business that maintains employment, that which reduces and that which increases employment, will at least maintain the existing level of total employment. If full employment exists, this will be maintained.

If full employment does not exist, there is no reason why business activity will not move to this level, because demand is guaranteed to equal any level of supply by management of rate of interest in the monetary system. If unemployment happens to be high because of a change from trade-cycle economics, a slight edge in favour of equity investment might be held for a time by keeping the rate of interest slightly lower than it should be. This would stimulate recovery, but it must not be allowed to persist when full employment approaches.

However, monetary management techniques have very little chance of working when the real value of money is not being maintained by eliminating cost inflation (through wage indexation) and maintaining a balance of payments on current account in international trade (through rates of exchange control). These are necessary parts of monetary management and vital to achieving an economic system that is fair to all.

Relationship to Other Theories

In classical economics, Say's Law said the supply created its own demand. This was true in barter and almost true with the early use of commodity money, but it certainly was not true once paper money and the use of bank credit were used to facilitate business activity. The modern use of money completely separated demand from supply, and the level of new activity was determined not by supply but by previous demand. When money demand differed from expectations at the time of resource supply, the new supply of resources was tailored to meet the changed demand expectations.

A shortfall in money demand meant lower profits, which in turn caused the use of productive resources to be reduced, lowering employment and living standards. Better than expected money demand meant higher profits, which in turn caused the use of productive resources to be increased, increasing employment and living standards. This trade cycle in the level of business activity has existed for several hundred years. It will continue to exist until we learn monetary management and make real and money demand always equal to any level of supply, including supply at the level of full employment.

Keynes regarded demand being equal to supply as a particular case that rarely, if ever, existed and his General Theory of Interest, Money and Employment tried to explain the shortfall of money demand. He proposed raising effective (money) demand by deficit spending in government budgets, and there are still many adherents to his doctrine. However, such methods have been tried and found wanting, because no one knows how much more demand is needed or when the right level has been found. Monetary management provides for demand to equal supply at all levels, all of the time—and at a constant real value for money so that the equilibrium is sustainable.

Friedmann's quantity of money theory was a well-meaning statistical exercise that got its logic all wrong and proved impossible things with figures. Monetary management shows that money and funds have no quantity, so there is not much point in pursuing monetary proposals. They never worked in practice. Manipulating rates of interest without knowing their true effect is absolutely disastrous to an economy.